→ BOOK I — C-Soprano or C-Tenor
BOOK II — F-Alto, F-Sopranino, F-Bass

THE BEST RECORDER METHOD YET

By ALBERT GAMSE

Charts, Exercises, Embellishments, Solos and Ensemble Music

The Recorder dates back several centuries. Master composers of the baroque era, including Bach, ̄ ̣mann, Purcell, etc., up to modern composers, have written ̣ ̣ ̣ ̣ ̣ble works for the instrument.

The popularity of the Recorder has be ̣ ̣ ̣ ing through the centuries and especially i ̣ ̣ ̣

Countless concerts all over the world have included ̣ ̣ ̣ ers, from the little Sopranino to the large Bass Recorders. Countless thousands of listeners became enthusiastic students.

We hope this book will be instrumental in creating and expanding musical interest and providing many hours of entertainment and enjoyment to player and listener alike.

THE PUBLISHER

"Govern these vents with your fingers and thumb, give it breath with your mouth, and it will discourse most eloquent music."
. . . . William Shakespeare (Hamlet)

"And thence I to Drumbleby's and did buy a recorder, the sound of it being, of all sounds in the world, most pleasing to me."
. . . . Samuel Pepys' Diary for April 8, 1668

CONTENTS

ENSEMBLE SELECTIONS

(Book 2, Alto, in Parentheses)

Page

Page

*NOTE—Except for selections starred * the
compositions on this page are from the
pens of popular composers of the 16th and
and 17th centuries, who have paid special
significance to music for flute and for
recorders.

**Ensemble arrangements of famous old
English tunes.

PLAYING THE RECORDER

TAKE CARE OF YOUR RECORDER

When first using it, take it apart and oil the inside of each part with a swab lightly dipped in woodwind oil. Some manufacturers recommend cleaning it with warm (not hot) water or with any mild disinfectant, like a mouth-wash. Most manufacturers supply instructions for the care of the specific instrument which you select. DO NOT OIL THE APERTURE (Opening) or the Fipple (plug fitting into mouthpiece).

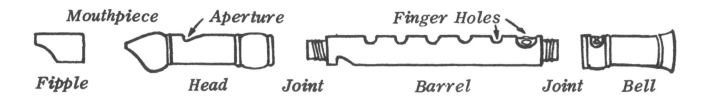

Let the oil dry overnight before playing. Hold it in your hands to keep it thoroughly warm. A new Recorder should be played only about 20 minutes a day for the first three or four days. After playing, wipe out the inside of each section with a dry swab (except the aperture and fipple) and let it dry completely. Moisture sometimes gathers in the narrow opening between the fipple and the mouthpiece, blurring the tone. If so, place the soft part of a fingertip over the aperture and blow sharply. Occasional cleaning (three or four times a year) is good for the preservation of the instrument.

THE FAMILY OF RECORDERS

Viewing the illustrations left to right:

1 BIG BASS (about 49" long)

2 BASS (about 36" long)

3 TENOR (about 25" long)

4 ALTO (about 18" long)

5 SOPRANO (or Descant) (about 12" long)

6 SOPRANINO (about 9" long)

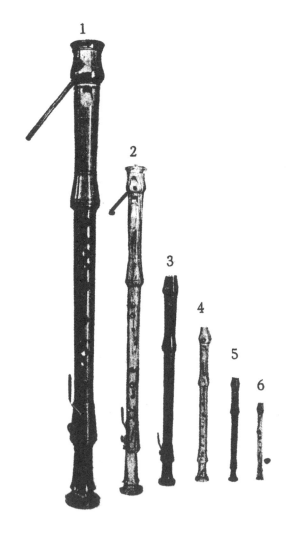

WRITTEN: SOUNDING:

The SOPRANO Recorder is pitched in C (its lowest note). It sounds an octave higher than written. It is very popular for school use and it is one of the lower priced instruments.

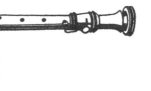

The TENOR Recorder is likewise pitched in C and it sounds as written. It is especially favored for ensemble playing. It is less desirable for solo playing than the Soprano or Alto recorders. A popular ensemble combines it with an alto and two sopranos.

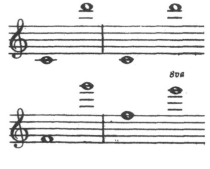

The SOPRANINO Recorder is the smallest member of the Recorder family. Its use and its available music is more limited, but it is favored for its size. It is pitched in F (F is its lowest note) and it sounds an octave higher than the written music.

The F-ALTO Recorder (sometimes called the "Treble" Recorder) is considered the most important member of the Recorder family, because much music was written expressly for this instrument. It is pitched in F (F being its lowest note) and it sounds as written.

The BASS Recorders are the largest members of the Recorder family. The standard Bass Recorder in F sounds an octave lower than the Alto. It is very effective for ensemble playing, for instance, in conjunction with two sopranos, an alto and a tenor.

The BIG BASS Recorder is pitched in C (C being its lowest note). It sounds an octave lower than the Tenor. It is wider and heavier than the standard BASS and it has a rich bass tone. It is chiefly used by advanced musicians.

WRITTEN   SOUNDING
8va

FINGERING (For both C and F Recorders)

The traditional, and most widely used, fingering of the Recorder is called "Baroque" (Old English). The German fingering was introduced about 25 years ago, with only two variations:

1. On the SOPRANO-TENOR RECORDERS, a variation in fingering F and F#
2. On the ALTO-SOPRANINO RECORDERS, a variation in fingering B and Bb

As you advance in your studies, you might try experimenting with the more modern German fingering to ascertain if it's more comfortable in some musical passages, but most players seem to prefer the Baroque fingering, especially in early grade studies.

Some Recorders are specifically designed to accommodate German fingering. They can be identified by hole 5, down from the mouthpiece. On English (Baroque) system Recorders, hole 5 is one of the largest holes; on German system Recorders, it is one of the smallest.

At this point, we suggest that you do not concern yourself with alternate fingerings, even though we have included alternates in our fingering charts (to the right of basic fingerings), until you have advanced to a stage where you can experiment in a relaxed manner and you feel quite at home with the fingering you have practiced.

In fingering your Recorder, it is not necessary to apply special pressure. The important thing is to place the fingers accurately. The Recorder player enjoys a greater ease of fingering than the player of a keyed instrument.

The following diagram illustrates how the fingers of each hand are numbered for reference purposes:

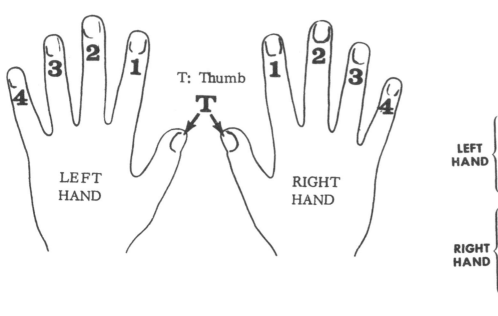

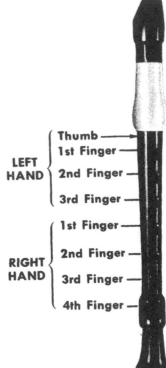

The Left Hand

The THUMB of the LEFT HAND is used to cover the hole in the back.

Fingers 1, 2 and 3 of the LEFT HAND are used to cover the 3 top holes.

The LITTLE FINGER of the LEFT HAND is NEVER USED.

The Right Hand

The THUMB of the RIGHT HAND fits on the thumb rest on back of the Recorder. It supports the Recorder.

Fingers 1 - 2 - 3 - 4 of the RIGHT HAND are used to cover the 4 lower holes.

General Comments

The FINGERING CHARTS which follow are designed for general reference purposes, as you advance in your studies. Do not attempt to memorize the charts, reserving your knowledge step by step to the tones individually introduced in this book. The general construction of the charts might be studied for future reference.

You will notice that WHITE CIRCLES are for the OPEN HOLES, BLACK CIRCLES are for the CLOSED HOLES, and BLACK & WHITE CIRCLES ARE PARTLY CLOSED HOLES. These are known as: Half Position Tones.

The upper tones are played with the thumb inserted half way into the indicated hole. The space to be left open and the amount of pressure by the thumb will vary with individual instruments. You will learn by experiment whether your instrument requires a larger or a smaller fraction of the hole left open and if the thumb should press lightly or heavily for tones in the upper register.

The end of the thumb is pressed into hole 1, leaving a small space above the nail. You may blow a little harder for tones in half position than for lower tones.

Some recorders are manufactured with small double holes in the right hand sections, 3rd and 4th fingers. In these cases, the charts indicate tones where both small holes are open or closed, or where one small hole is left open.

CONCERNING THE MUSIC

Following the fingering charts, you will find a brief analysis of the fundamental things you would be wise in learning about music notation. If you do not already read music, these rudiments will assist you in associating the printed tones with the Recorder holes which are to be fingered.

Tunes in this book are presented progressively for SOLO playing, starting with the early "toots", leading to ensemble playing. Solo tunes for the F Alto Recorder (Book II) were arranged 2-1/2 tones higher than for the same tunes for C Soprano Recorder. However, where ensemble playing requires a combination of Soprano and Alto, all parts have been arranged in uniform keys, the easiest for everyone concerned.

Naturally, the fingering of the C Soprano notes (as you can see from the Charts) will vary from the fingering of the same tones for the F Alto notes.

Alto players will be able to play solos and duets, in some instances, by transposing the music an octave higher.

HOLDING THE RECORDER

1. RIGHT HAND picks up the Recorder at the bottom.

2. LEFT HAND THUMB covers thumb hole at rear.

3. Using cushion part (not tips) of fingers 1-2, cover holes 1-2 at top of Recorder with LEFT HAND.

4. Balance the Recorder at rear with RIGHT HAND THUMB, between holes 4-5 from the top.

5. The fingers should be slightly curved. Do not raise your fingers more than 1/2" above the holes. Your arms should be at a comfortable angle away from your body.

6. Your first notes are played by covering the upper holes with LEFT HAND fingers, using the RIGHT HAND only to steady the instrument.

7. Whether sitting or standing, correct posture is important. Stand or sit erect with head up; arms, hands and fingers should be relaxed without stiffness.

8. Use the RIGHT HAND to cover holes 5-6-7-8. Thus, the Recorder is held firmly between the thumb and the little finger of the right hand, steadied against the lips. These are the ONLY FINGERS used to steady the Recorder. Other fingers, when not covering holes, should not rest on the Recorder, but held poised slightly above the holes, being prepared to cover them.

9. In covering the holes (except where HALF-COVERING is indicated) no air must escape around the edge of the hole. Even the slightest escape of air will alter the pitch and produce a poor tone.

10. Hold the Recorder in a DIAGONAL POSITION (a 45 degree angle down from the body. It should not rest against the knee when you play in a seated position. Your arms should hang relaxed and loosely away from the body, avoiding the tension of holding them tightly against the body or extending elbows too widely.

11. The Recorder is held between the lips but not too far inside the mouth.

BLOWING, TONGUING and BREATHING

The mouthpiece is held about 1/4" covered by the lips. It should not touch your teeth. To blow the recorder, you need very little breath and practically no muscular lip control. A smooth tone requires good breath control. Blow gently.

Tones have to be TONGUED to give them a clean-cut sound. The tongue is moved from the upper part of the mouth downward, opening a passage for the breath that carries the tone, and again upwards when the tone ends.

Fingers and tongue must move in strict coordination. The fingers come down with a light hammer touch and held tight for the duration of the notes, and quickly released.

To start a note, use your tongue, saying "du". This is called tonguing.

To close a note, bring your tongue against your teeth for the sound of "d" unpronounced.

The higher notes require a soft "tu" at every blowing. The syllable "tut" will produce a crisp "staccato" (a short sharp sound) at every blowing.

An important requirement is to maintain an even pressure of blowing for the duration of each tone. The lowest tones need a very little amount of breath. A little more pressure is applied with every step upward.

Tonguing is not necessary in certain slurred notes and quick passages. Fast tone repetitions are sometimes played with "double tonguing" like in saying "ticky ticky ticky".

A comma-like symbol ' is used in some recorder music to indicate a quick breath, without losing the tempo. You can stop the sound by placing the tongue to the roof of the mouth, thereby stopping the air flow. Inhale whenever you see a breath mark.

The high notes of most recorders need a little more wind than the low notes. So, when notes go higher, so does the breath pressure — and down when the notes come down.

OF UTMOST IMPORTANCE! Each finger should play only the indicated holes. When a finger is not in use, it should be held directly over the hole.

FINGERING CHART

CHART 1 -
Lower Octave

FINGERING CHART
For Baroque and German Fingered Recorders

○ Open Hole   ● Closed Hole   ◐ ◑ Partly Closed Hole   ◉ Double Hole, One Closed

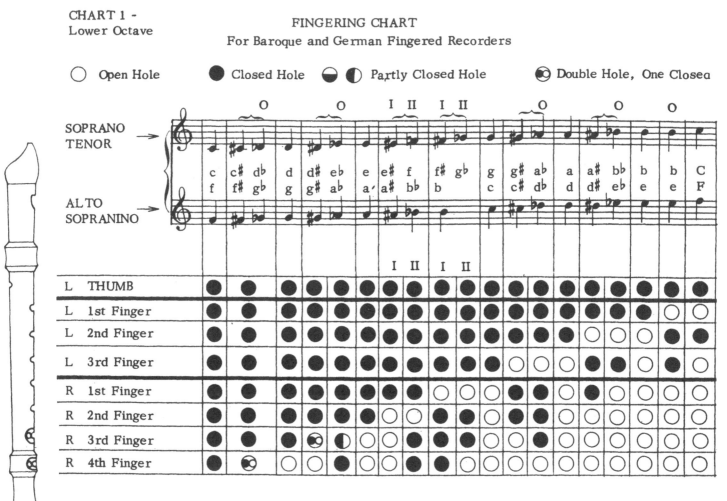

	c / f	c# / f# db / gb	d / g	d# / g# eb / ab	e / a' e# / a# f / bb	f# / b gb	g / c	g# / c# ab / db	a / d	a# / d# bb / eb	b / e	b / e	C / F
L THUMB	●	●	● ●	● ●	● ● ●	● ●	●	● ●	●	● ●	●	●	●
L 1st Finger	●	●	● ●	● ●	● ● ●	● ●	●	● ●	●	● ●	●	○	○
L 2nd Finger	●	●	● ●	● ●	● ● ●	● ●	●	● ●	●	○ ○	○	●	●
L 3rd Finger	●	●	● ●	● ●	● ● ●	● ●	●	○ ○	○	● ○	○	●	○
R 1st Finger	●	●	● ●	● ●	● ● ●	○ ○	●	● ●	○	○ ○	○	○	○
R 2nd Finger	●	●	● ●	● ●	● ○	○ ●	●	○ ●	●	○ ○	○	○	○
R 3rd Finger	●	●	● ◉	◑ ○	○ ○ ●	● ●	●	○ ○	○	○ ○	○	○	○
R 4th Finger	●	◉	○ ○	● ○	● ○ ●	● ●	○	○ ○	○	○ ○	○	○	○

I - German Fingering   II - Baroque Fingering

O — Optional Fingering

L - Left Hand   R - Right Hand

NOTE 1 - It is not necessary to study these charts in advance.   They will be useful after you have
made progress with individual fingering lessons in this book.

NOTE 2 - These charts are applicable to the BASS RECORDER by lowering the F Scale (Alto) 1 octave.

NOTE 3 - The columns connected by ⌒ represent the same sound, expressed in two ways.   For
example C# and Db are one and the same tones.

CHART 2 -
Higher Octave

○ Open Hole   ● Closed Hole   ◐ Partly Closed Hole   ⊙ Double Hole, One Closed

Top staff markings: O   O   O   I   II   I   II   O

SOPRANO / TENOR → (treble staff)

ALTO / SOPRANINO → (treble staff, 8va)

	C F	C# F#	Db Gb	D G	D# G#	Eb Ab	E A	E A	E# A#	F Bb	F# B	Gb B	G C	G# C#	Ab Db	A D	A# D#	Bb Eb	B E	C F
									I	II	I	II								
L THUMB	●	●	○	○	○	○	○	◐	◐	◐	◐	◐	◐	◐	◐	◐	◐	◐	◐	◐
L 1st Finger	○	○	○	●	○	○	○	●	●	●	●	●	●	●	●	●	●		●	●
L 2nd Finger	●	○	●	●	●	●	●	●	●	●	●	●	●	●	●	●	●	●	●	○
L 3rd Finger	○	○	●	○	○	●	●	●	●	●	●	●	●	●	○	●	○	○	○	○
R 1st Finger	○	○	○	○	○	●	●	●	●	●	○	○	●	●	○	○	●		●	●
R 2nd Finger	○	○	○	○	○	●	●	●	○	○	●	●	●	○	●	○	●		●	●
R 3rd Finger	○	○	○	○	○	●	○	○	○	○	●	○	○	○	●	○	●		○	○
R 4th Finger	○	○	○	○	○	○	○	○	○	○	●	○	○	●	○	○	○		○	○

I - German Fingering   II - Baroque Fingering

O — Optional Fingering

L - Left Hand   R - Right Hand

ELEMENTARY MUSIC PRINCIPLES

THE STAFF.   All music notes are placed on a STAFF-through the lines or in the spaces between the lines.   The bottom line is referred to as Line 1, the bottom space -space 1.

THE "G-CLEF" is placed at the beginning of a Staff.   It is called a "G-Clef" simply because it encircles Line 2 (which, you will later learn, is used for music note "G").

MUSIC NOTES.   In paragraph "Timing", you will note various kinds of music notes.   In the illustrations below, we show "whole notes".

NOTES ON LINES:

E   G   B   D   F

IN SPACES:

F   A   C   E

Memory aid: Every good boy does   fine.

LINES AND SPACES:

E   F   G   A   B   C   D   E   F

LEGER LINES AND SPACES.   These will show notes extending below and above the staff (in alphabetic sequence):

C   D   G   A

BAR LINES.   These are vertical lines crossing the staff, as illustrated:

The space between two bar lines is a MEASURE, which divides music into equal Time Units.   The double bar terminates a specific section of the piece and sometimes will be found at the beginning of a piece.   A single bar plus a heavy bar indicates the con-clusion of the piece.

TIMING (duration of the music notes).

Music is divided into "time units".   A "time signature" is indicated at the beginning of a piece, like these: $\frac{2}{4}$ $\frac{3}{4}$ $\frac{6}{8}$ $\frac{4}{4}$ * C

The TOP numbers show number of beats to a measure.   The BOTTOM numbers show the "time value" of each beat, as follows:

WHOLE NOTE   o   4 beats

HALF NOTE   ♩   2 beats

QUARTER NOTE   ♩   1 beat

* $\frac{4}{4}$ and C are synomymous com-mon time indicators. If C has a vertical line through it: ¢ it means "Cut Time", play faster.

EIGHTH NOTE  or ♪ receives 1/2 beat. It takes two 8th notes to give the same time duration as one quarter note.

Groups of 8th notes are usually printed with "beams", like this:

We now show how time is counted. Suppose the piece is in 4/4 time. A WHOLE NOTE would fill the entire measure and receive the count of 1-2-3-4. It would take two HALF NOTES to produce the same count. The following illustrates the counting principle:

COUNT: 1 2 3 4   1 - 2 3 - 4   1   2   3   4   1 & 2 & 3 & 4 &
                                                            (and)

Each note has an equivalent (silent) REST:

Whole   Half   Quarter   Eighth
rest   rest   rest   rest

A dot after a note raises its time value by 1/2. Thus, a dotted half note ♩· is held for 3 counts.

TIES. If two of the same notes are tied by a mark like this ⌣ or ⌢ , hold the same note for the full time value of both.

ACCIDENTALS. Occasions arise when notes must be altered in pitch. This is done by signs which are called "Accidentals", as follows:

♯ A "sharp" sign. It raises the pitch of a note by 1/2 step.
♭ A "flat" sign. It lowers the pitch of a note by 1/2 step.
♮ A "natural" sign. It cancels a previous sharp or flat sign.

When an "accidental" is placed before a note, it is valid throughout the measure. For instance, if a sharp is placed before a C in a measure, any other C in that measure is raised 1/2 step unless it is cancelled by a natural sign.

KEY SIGNATURES.

A "key signature" is used in music to indicate the pitch of the notes - throughout the entire selection. If there is no "key signature", it means that the piece is in the Key of C, without any sharps or flats, except as might arise as "accidentals". Otherwise, the key signature appears at the beginning of the staff, between the G Clef sign and the "time signature". It consists of one or more sharps, or one or more flats. These sharps or flats indicate that the notes which they represent are to be raised or lowered in pitch THROUGHOUT THE ENTIRE PIECE.

All F's are played as F♯ throughout the piece:

All B's are played as B♭ throughout the piece:

All B's and E's are played B♭ and E♭ throughout the piece:

REPEAT SIGN. A "Repeat Sign" is a pair of dots, one over the other like a colon, placed on the staff before or after a double bar, like this:

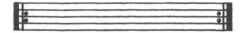

This indicates a section of the piece which is played and then repeated. If there's but one repeat sign (the 2nd in above illustration), it means repeat from the beginning of a piece or a specific section thereof. This is usually indicated by a sign 𝄋 for example, DS 𝄋 al Fine, means - Del Signo (from the Sign) to the designated end (Fine).

OCTAVES. An Octave is the distance from a lower tone to the same tone higher in pitch.

Sample octaves are illustrated:

Octave, low C to high C: Octave, low F to high F:

Octave, low D to high D: Octave, low G to high G:

STACCATO. You will sometimes see a light dot above or below a note. This means that the note is played "staccato", that is, lightly and crisply. (When the stem points up, the dot goes below the head of the note.)

PICK-UP NOTE(S).

You will occasionally see one or more notes before the opening measure of a selection which do not total the designated value of a full measure.

They are called "pick-up notes. The time needed to complete the value of a measure is compensated at the end of the piece, since every measure of the piece should have a specific number of beats.

For example, if there is a pick-up note in a measure of 4/4 time (and if it happens that it's a quarter note), you will only see 3 quarter notes at the end of the piece instead of 4 quarter notes, because you had to compensate for the pick-up note at the beginning.

CHORDS.

A "chord" is a harmonious combination of notes. We are here dealing with a melody instrument. The chord names above the melody lines, which you will find in much of the music in this book are used for accompaniment by piano, guitar, autoharp, etc.

DYNAMICS.

The suggestions for the speed and loudness of a piece are partially indicated:

Andante - "slow"   *pp*   "very soft"
Moderato - "moderate"   *p*   "soft"
Allegro - "fast"   *mf*   "moderately loud"
                                                    f   "loud"

FIRST TOOTS WITH B

B

Cover holes with Thumb and Finger 1 of Left Hand.

❋ Comma **,** means "Take a breath".

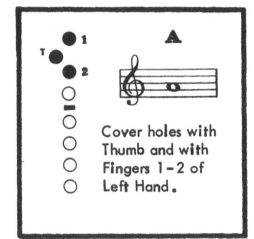

A

Cover holes with Thumb and with Fingers 1-2 of Left Hand.

FIRST TOOTS WITH A

FIRST TOOTS WITH B and A

FIRST TOOTS WITH G

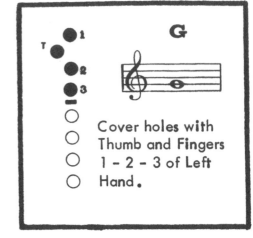

Cover holes with Thumb and Fingers 1 - 2 - 3 of Left Hand.

Count   1 2 3   1 2 3   1 2 3   1 2 3

Count   1   2   3   4   1   2   3   4   1   2   3   4   1   2   3   4

FIRST TOOTS WITH B-A-G

Count   1   2   3   4   1   2   3   4   1   2   3   4   1   2   3   4

1   2   3   4   1   2   3   4   1   2   3   4   1   2   3   4

MARY HAD A LITTLE LAMB

Count   1   2   3   4   1   2   3   4   1   2   3   4   1   2   3   4

1   2   3   4   1   2   3   4   1   2   3   4   1   2   3   4

FIRST TOOTS WITH HIGH C

Count: 1 2 3 4   1 2 3 4   1 2 3 4   1 2 3 4

FIRST TOOTS WITH A-B-C-G

Count: 1 2 3 4   1 2 3 4   1 2 3 4   1 2 3 4

1 2 3 4   1 2 3 4   1 2 3 4   1 2 3 4

GOOD-NIGHT, LADIES

Count: 1 2 3 4   1 2 3 4   1 2 3 4   1 2 3 4

1 2 3 4   1 2 3 4   1 2 3 4   1 2 3 4

FIRST TOOTS WITH HIGH D

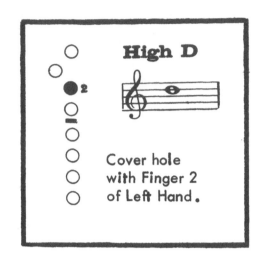

High D

Cover hole
with Finger 2
of Left Hand.

FIRST TOOTS WITH G-A-B-C-D

PARTY POLKA

THE CUCKOO

Count   3   1 2 3   1 2 3   1 2 3   1 2 3   1 2 3   1 2 3   1 2 3

"pick up"

1 2 3   1 2 3   1 2 3   1 2 3   1 2 3   1 2 3   1 2 3   1 2

(the 3rd count
was in the "pick
up")

SLEEP, BABY, SLEEP

Count   1 2 3 4   1 2 3 4   1 2 3 4   1 2 3 4   1 2 3 4   1 2 3 4

1 2 3 4   1 2 3 4   1 2 3 4   1 2 3 4

AUNT RHODY

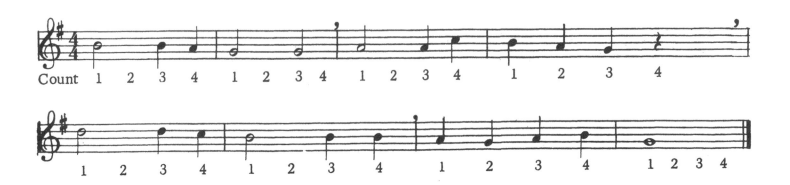

Count   1 2 3 4   1 2 3 4   1 2 3 4   1 2 3 4

1 2 3 4   1 2 3 4   1 2 3 4   1 2 3 4

We introduce here "Chord Names" above the melody lines.   These are for ACCOMPANIMENT only, by chorded instruments, such as Piano, Organ, Autoharp, &c.

JINGLE BELLS

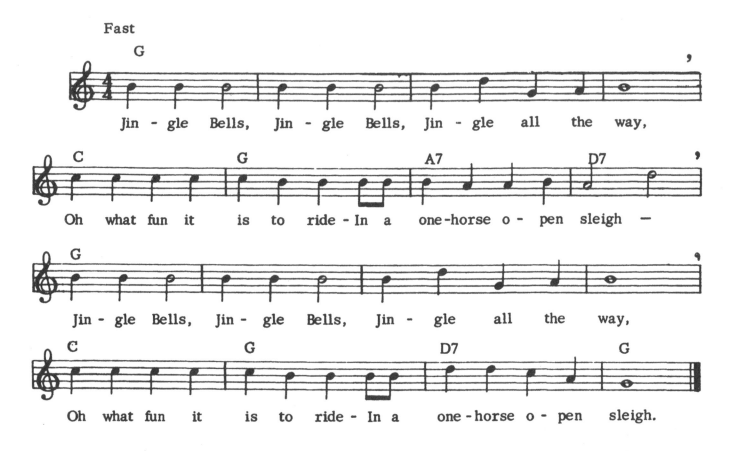

Jin - gle Bells, Jin - gle Bells, Jin - gle all the way,

Oh what fun it is to ride - In a one-horse o - pen sleigh —

Jin - gle Bells, Jin - gle Bells, Jin - gle all the way,

Oh what fun it is to ride - In a one-horse o - pen sleigh.

WHEN THE SAINTS GO MARCHING IN

Oh! When The Saints Go March - ing In,

Oh! When The Saints Go March - ing In,

Oh! I want to be in that num - ber,

When The Saints Go March - ing In! _____

FIRST TOOTS WITH F

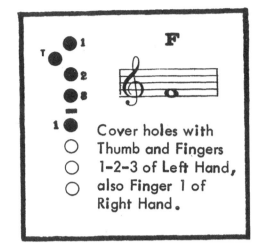

F

Cover holes with
Thumb and Fingers
1-2-3 of Left Hand,
also Finger 1 of
Right Hand.

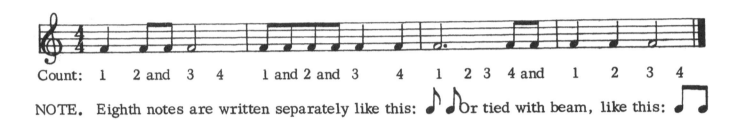

Count: 1   2 and 3   4   1 and 2 and 3   4   1 2 3 4 and   1   2   3   4

NOTE. Eighth notes are written separately like this: ♪ ♪ or tied with beam, like this: ♫

FIRST TOOTS WITH F-G-A-B-C-D

EXERCISE USING F THROUGH HIGH D

FIRST TOOTS WITH E

FIRST TOOTS WITH E THROUGH HIGH D

* This is a "Repeat" Sign.
See Fundamentals.

CONSTRUCTION OF FIRST CHORDS

(Arpeggio Chords, meaning single successive notes)

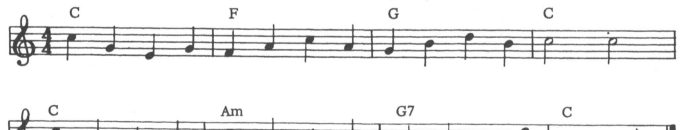

MARTHA

(Theme)

Moderate dance tempo

Friedrich Von Flotow

* This piece has a 1st and a 2nd ending. Play through 1, repeat. On the repeat, however,
  you skip the measures bracketed as 1, and instead, play the measures bracketed as 2.

JULIDA POLKA

Bright polka

PLAYING LOW D

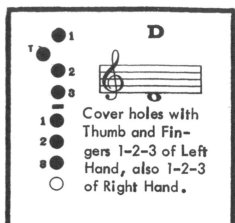

D

Cover holes with Thumb and Fingers 1-2-3 of Left Hand, also 1-2-3 of Right Hand.

OLD MacDONALD

Brightly

* Accent mark   means: Note is sharper, crisper.

EXERCISE USING LOW D THROUGH HIGH D

Cover holes with
Thumb and Fin-
gers 1-2-3 of
Left Hand, also
1-2-3-4 Right.

PLAYING LOW C

THE C-MAJOR SCALE

A Scale is a series of tones forming the familiar "do re mi fa sol la ti do".

THIS OLD MAN

ON TOP OF OLD SMOKY

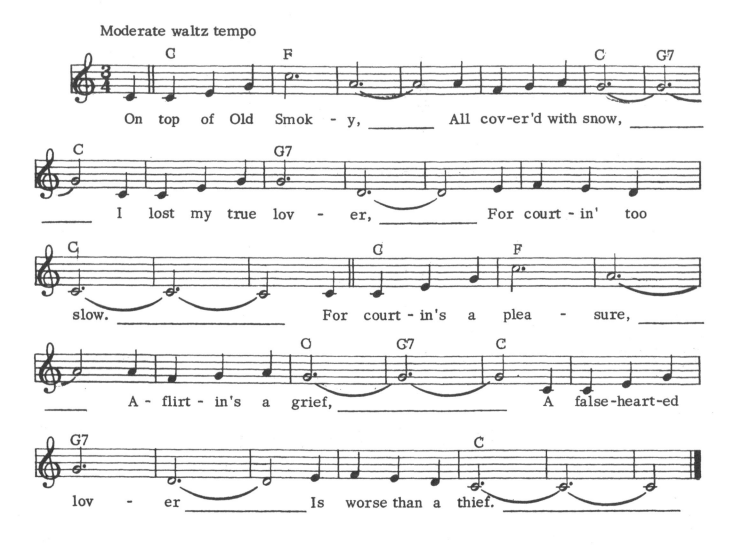

Moderate waltz tempo

On top of Old Smok - y, _____ All cov-er'd with snow, _____

_____ I lost my true lov - er, _____ For court - in' too

slow. _____ For court - in's a plea - sure, _____

_____ A - flirt - in's a grief, _____ A false-heart-ed

lov - er _____ Is worse than a thief. _____

THE CAMPTOWN RACES

Camp-town la-dies sing this song: Doo-dah, doo-dah! Camptown track is

nine miles long, Oh doo-da day. Gwine to run all night, Gwine to run all

day, I bet my mon-ey on the bob tail nag, Some-bod-y won on the bay.

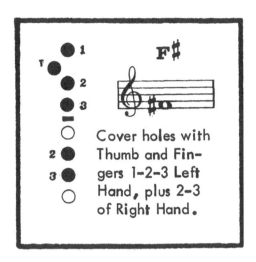

PLAYING F#

NOTE the F# in the key signature.   It governs every F in the music, which becomes F Sharp (F#).

NEW CHORDS

* This F is preceded by a natural sign, dissolving the sharp #
** Now the sharp is re-instituted.

PRACTICE EXERCISE USING ALL NOTES

DON'T FORGET! When a flat (♭) appears on the B line, at the beginning of the staff, it means you are in the Key of F, and every B in the key of F is actually B♭ (B Flat).

See FINGERING CHART on Page 8 for optional fingering of the B Flat tone.

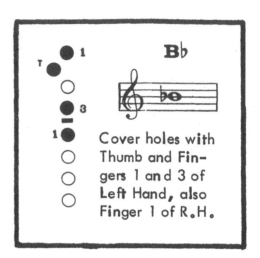

B♭

Cover holes with Thumb and Fingers 1 and 3 of Left Hand, also Finger 1 of R.H.

PLAYING B♭

NEW CHORDS

(In "arpeggio" single note form)

AMERICA

My coun - try, 'tis of thee, Sweet land of li - ber - ty, Of thee I

sing.   Land where my fa - thers died, Land of the pil - grim's pride,

From ev - ry - moun - tain-side, Let - free - dom ring.

IN THE GLOAMING

Moderately

Ored - Harrison

In the gloam-ing, Oh my dar - ling, when the lights are dim and low, And the qui - et shad - ows fall - ing soft - ly come and soft - ly go. Where the winds are sob - bing - faint - ly, with a gen - tle un - known - woe, Will you think of me and love me, As you did once long a - go.

LONG LONG AGO

Moderately

Thomas Bayly

Tell me the tales that to me were so dear, Long long a - go, Long long a - go. Sing me the songs I de - light - ed to hear, Long long a - go, long a - go! (Fine)

DS 𝄋 al Fine

New Note-High E

TWINKLE, TWINKLE, LITTLE STAR

Moderately

IT CAME UPON A MIDNIGHT CLEAR

Moderately

Sears - Willis

MY WILD IRISH ROSE

Moderate Waltz

Chauncey Olcott

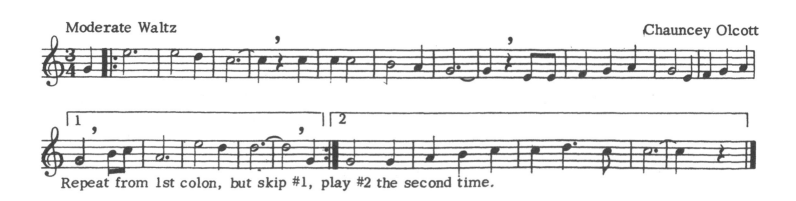

Repeat from 1st colon, but skip #1, play #2 the second time.

New Note-High F

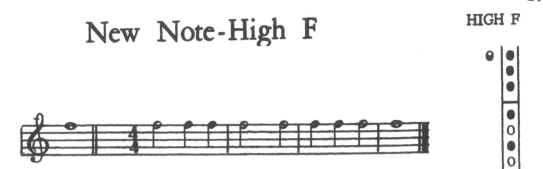

HIGH F

SILENT NIGHT

This is one of several selections in which we show individual diagrams for easier sight-reading.

Mohr-Gruber

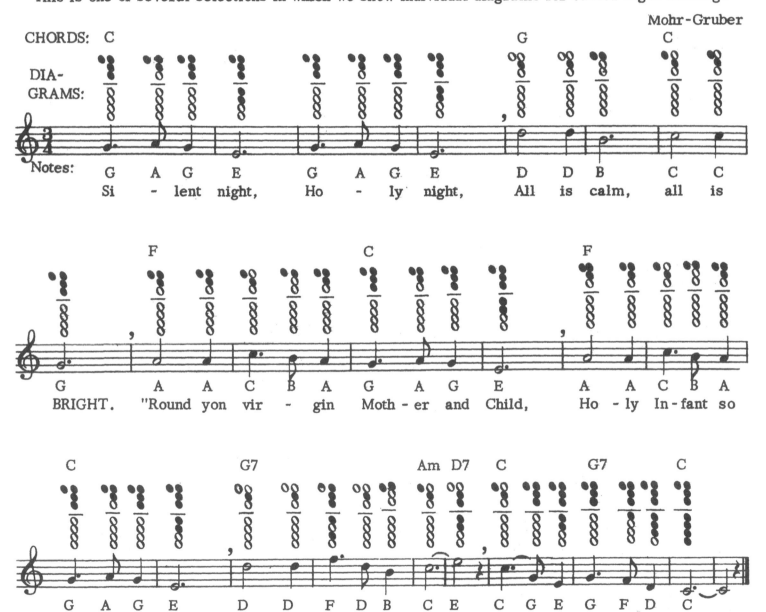

The music on this page is in the Key of G, identified by a sharp (♯) sign on upper F line, which affects every F in the music, low F or high F.   All F's are F♯ unless cancelled by natural sign (♮).   In "Daisy Bell" we show the ♯ before each F, but hereafter it must be remembered.

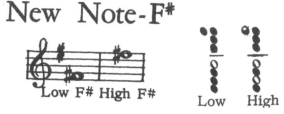

A BICYCLE BUILT FOR TWO

Moderate waltz

By Henry Dacre

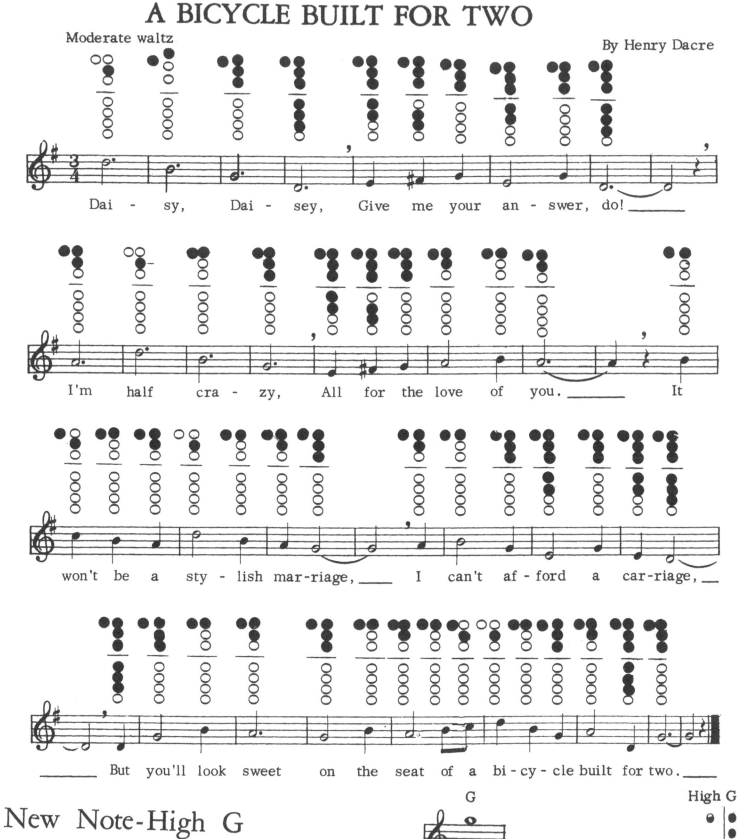

Dai - sy, Dai - sey, Give me your an - swer, do!_____

I'm half cra - zy, All for the love of you._____ It

won't be a sty - lish mar-riage,____ I can't af - ford a car-riage,__

_____ But you'll look sweet on the seat of a bi - cy - cle built for two.____

New Note-High G

SCALE IN G MAJOR

AFTER THE BALL

Moderate waltz   Charles K. Harris

Af - -ter the ball is o - ver, Af - ter the break of morn,__

_____ Af - ter the danc - ers leav - ing, Af - ter the

stars are gone, Man - y a heart is ach - ing,

If you could read them all,_____ Man - y the

hopes that have van - ished, Af - ter the ball.____

The Key of D

The key of D is identified by TWO SHARPS, F♯ and C♯. Throughout the music, F and C are played F♯ and C♯. Practice a few measures with the new notes and the scale of D major:

D E F♯ G A B C♯ D

PAPER ROSES

Slowly with expression

Torre - Spielman

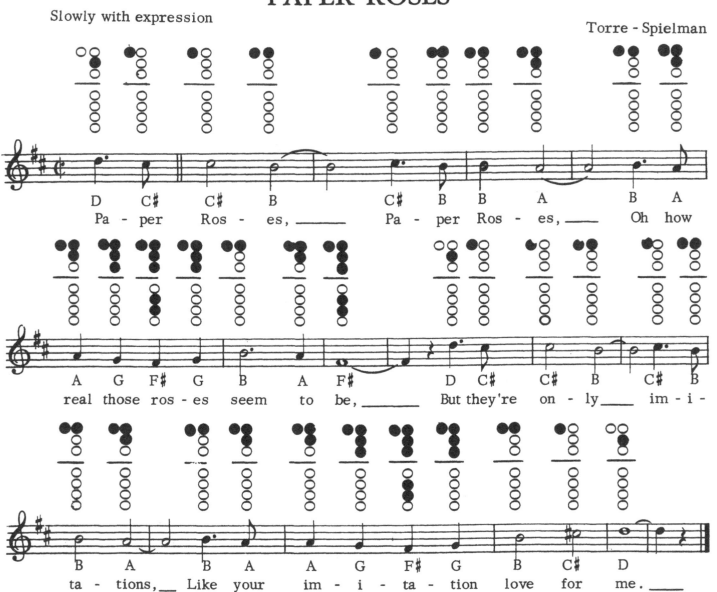

©MCMLX by Pambill Music Inc., assigned MCMLXII to
Lewis Music Publishing Co., Inc.

BIRTHDAY THEME

The Key of B♭ Major

The key of B♭ Major is identified by 2 flats, on the B line and in the E space. Any B or E in the piece automatically becomes B♭ and E♭ without the necessity of a flat (♭) sign before the notes. This key introduces 4 new notes for your recorder:

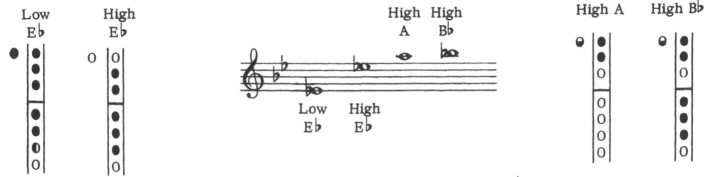

EXERCISES FOR ALL NEW NOTES — AND SCALE IN KEY OF B♭

GLORY, GLORY, HALLELUJAH

We continue, in this piece, to show the individual flat signs.

NOTE. - After this, you're "on your own" to flat each B and E in the Key of B♭, unless naturalized by the sign ♮ .

IN THE GOOD OLD SUMMER TIME

Moderate waltz

Shields - Evans

In the good old Sum - mer - time, _____ In the good old
Sum - mer - time. _____ Stroll - ing through the shad - y lanes
with your "ba - by mine". _____ You hold her hand and
she holds yours, And that's a ver - y good sign _____ That she's your
toot - sie woot - sie in the good old Sum - mer - time. _____

DOWN BY THE STATION

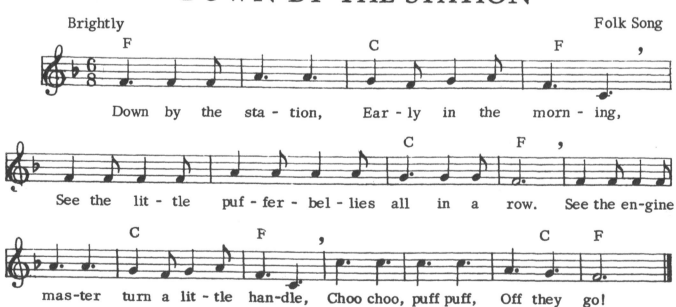

Brightly

Folk Song

Down by the sta - tion, Ear - ly in the morn - ing,
See the lit - tle puf - fer - bel - lies all in a row. See the en-gine
mas - ter turn a lit - tle han-dle, Choo choo, puff puff, Off they go!

The Key of E♭

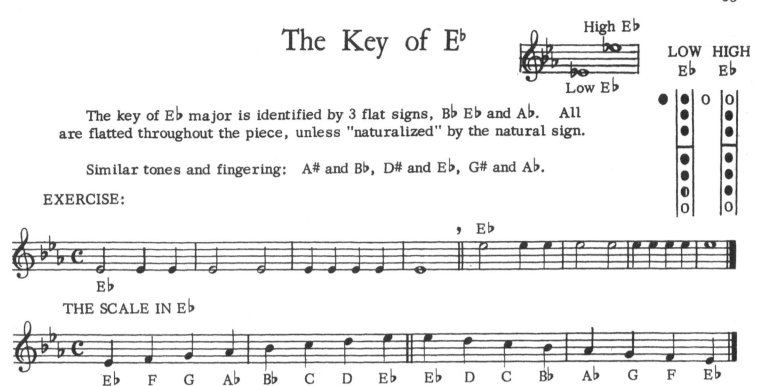

The key of E♭ major is identified by 3 flat signs, B♭ E♭ and A♭.   All
are flatted throughout the piece, unless "naturalized" by the natural sign.

Similar tones and fingering: A# and B♭, D# and E♭, G# and A♭.

MELODY IN E♭

BILL BAILEY
(Won't You Please Come Home?)

Moderately

HUGHIE CANNON

Won't you come home, Bill Bai - ley, won't you come home?

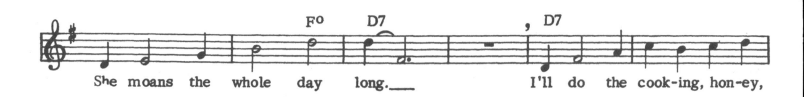

She moans the whole day long.___ I'll do the cook-ing, hon-ey,

I'll pay the rent, I know I've done you wrong.___

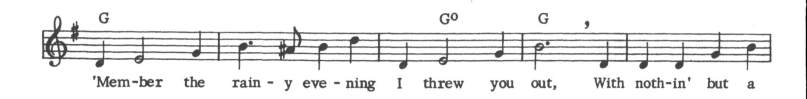

'Mem-ber the rain - y eve - ning I threw you out, With noth-in' but a

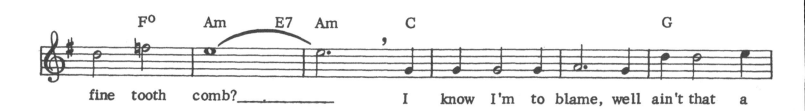

fine tooth comb?___ I know I'm to blame, well ain't that a

shame? Bill Bai - ley, won't you please come home?___

GYPSY LOVE SONG

Words by
HARRY SMITH

Music by
VICTOR HERBERT

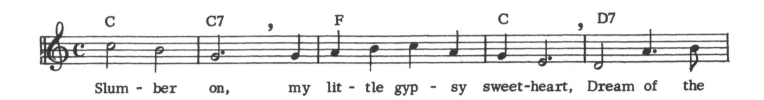

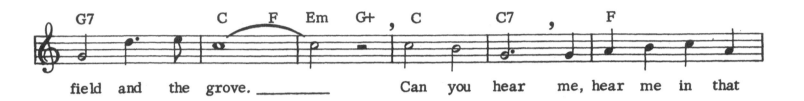

Slum - ber on, my lit - tle gyp - sy sweet-heart, Dream of the

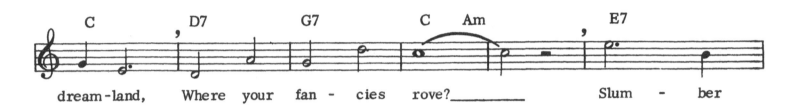

field and the grove. _____ Can you hear me, hear me in that

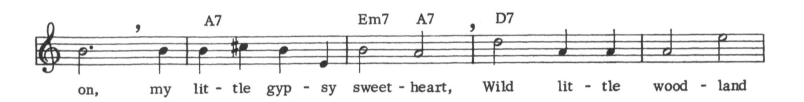

dream-land, Where your fan - cies rove? _____ Slum - ber

on, my lit - tle gyp - sy sweet - heart, Wild lit - tle wood - land

dove. _____ Can you hear the song ___ that ___ tells you,

All my ___ heart's true love? _____

THE SIDEWALKS OF NEW YORK

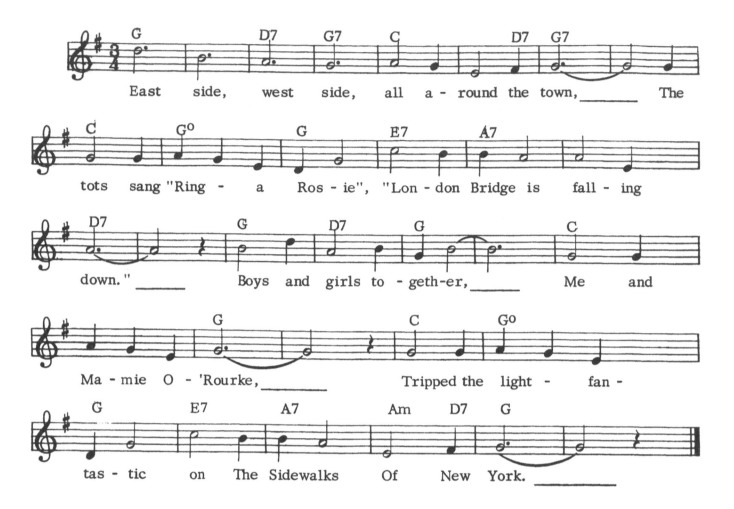

LITTLE ANNIE ROONEY

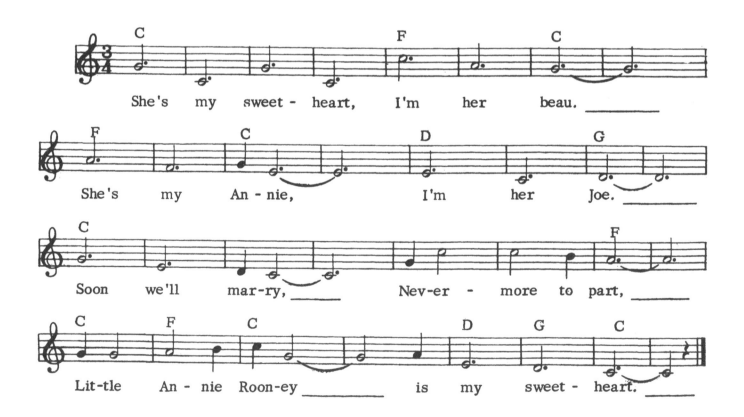

RED RIVER VALLEY

HOME ON THE RANGE

VALSETTE
(15th Century German)

Valse moderato

THE TOBACCO SHOP
(Traditional French)

Allegretto

J'ai du bon ta - bac dans ma ta - ba - tiè - re, J'ai du bon ta - bac, tu m'en auras pas.

J'en ai du fin et du-ra - té, Ce n'est_pas pour ton vi-lain nez.

J'ai du bon ta-bac dans ma ta-ba - tie - re, J'ai du bon ta-bac tu m'en au-ras pas.

FOLK DANCE
(French)

Allegro

CHORALE
(Bach)

Moderato

FOLK DANCE
(16th Century English)

Allegro

A HAPPY FEELING
(16th Century German)

Allegro

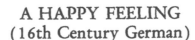

SWEET SPRINGTIME
(Traditional French)

Moderato

AN OLD GERMAN DANCE

Valse allegretto

FROM A MOZART SONATA
(Theme)

Moderato

GAVOTTE
(Michael Praetorius)

Gavotte moderato

AN OLD SWEDISH DANCE

GARDEN GREENERY
(16th Century English)

MINUET
(James Hook)

A PLEASANT THOUGHT
(From a Bach Chorale)

A GENTLE BREEZE
(Old German Dance)

BE GLAD, MY SOUL
(Bach)

It has been pointed out in the chapter on PLAYING INSTRUCTIONS that F-Alto Recorder has "F" for its lowest note and it sounds as written. Whereas, the Soprano Recorder has "C" for its lowest note and sounds an octave higher than written.

Therefore, if an Alto Recorder player is desirous of playing music which is written below F, it becomes possible by merely transposing the melody an octave higher.

A group of songs follows in which this transposition to the higher octave has been included for the Alto Recorder in the music. As a result, the compositions are playable by the Soprano Recorder solo, by the Alto Recorder solo, or by both together. When played together, it will not result in a HARMONY DUET but rather in UNISON, meaning that both instruments are playing the same notes.

AMAZING GRACE

Text: John Newton

Adaptation: Bernard Gasso

2. 'Twas grace that taught my heart to fear
    And grace my fears relieved.
    How precious did that grace appear
    The hour I first believed.

3. Through many dangers, toils and snares
    I have already come.
    'Tis grace hath brought me safe this far
    And grace will lead me home.

4. When we've been there ten thousand years,
    Bright shining as the sun.
    We've no less days to sing God's praise
    Than when we first begun.

SCARBOROUGH FAIR

English Folk Song
New lyrics by Albert Gamse

2.
Have him make me a cambric shirt,
Parsley, sage, rosemary and thyme,
Without a seam or fine needle work,
And then he'll be a true love of mine.

3.
Have him wash it in yonder dry well,
Parsley, sage, rosemary and thyme,
Where ne'er a drop of water e'er fell,
And then he'll be a true love of mine.

4.
Have him find me an acre of land,
Parsley, sage, rosemary and thyme,
Between the sea and over the sand,
And then he'll be a true love of mine.

5.
Plow the land with the horn of a lamb,
Parsley, sage, rosemary and thyme,
Then sow some seeds from north of the dam
And then he'll be a true love of mine.

6.
If he tells me he can't, I'll reply:
Parsley, sage, rosemary and thyme,
Let me know that at least he will try,
And then he'll be a true love of mine.

7.
Love imposes impossible tasks,
Parsley, sage, rosemary and thyme,
Though not more than any heart asks!
And I must know he's a true love of mine.

8.
Dear, when thou hast finished thy task,
Parsley, sage, rosemary and thyme,
Come to me, my hand for to ask,
For thou then art a true love of mine!

O SUSANNA

By STEPHEN FOSTER

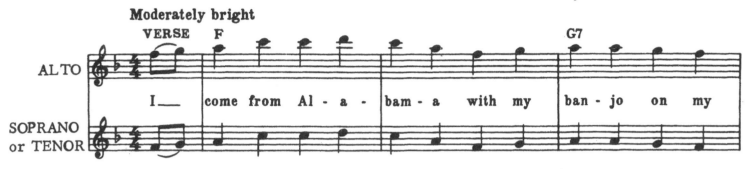

HE'S GOT THE WHOLE WORLD
IN HIS HANDS

Spiritual

2. He's got the land and sea in His hands;
   He's got the wind and rain in His hands;
   He's got the spring and fall in His hands;
   He's got the whole world in His hands.
      Chorus:

3. He's got the young and old in His hands;
   He's got the rich and poor in His hands;
   Yes, He's got ev'ryone in His hands;
   He's got the whole world in His hands.
      Chorus:

HAVAH NAGILAH

Words (English):
Albert Gamse

ISRAELI FOLK SONG

LA BAMBA

American version by Albert Gamse

Moderately

WEST INDIAN DANCE

GREENSLEEVES

ENGLISH TRADITIONAL

2. I bought thee petticoats of the best,
   The cloth as fine as a cloth could be,
   I gave thee jewels to fill thy chest,
   And all this I spent for the love of thee.

   (Chorus)

3. Oh Lady Greensleeves, farewell, adieu!
   I pray the good Lord may prosper thee,
   For I am always thy love so true,
   Till you return for to love but me.

   (Chorus)

WHEN JOHNNY COMES MARCHING HOME

March tempo

TRADITIONAL

2. When Johnny comes marching home again,
    We'll sing once more.
    The heart will recall the morning when
    He went to war.
    With a song we'll proudly proclaim that he
    Has fought for keeping this nation free,
    On that great great day,
    When Johnny comes marching home.

DUETS FOR TWO SOPRANOS
(Or Soprano and Tenor)

THE TIRED HEART

THOMAS CAMPION
1567-1620

ROSEBUDS

WILLIAM LAWES
(17th Century)

MAY I COME TO THEE?

THOMAS CAMPION
1567-1620

SPRIGHTLY LILLIAN

TRADITIONAL
(18th Century)

SILESIAN DANCE

OLD GERMAN LULLABY

JOY TO THE WORLD

Brightly

GEORGE FRIEDRICH HANDEL

58

GAVOTTE

GEORGE FRIEDRICH HANDEL

MINUETTO

TELEMANN

THE KERRY DANCERS

IRISH DANCE

AMERICA, THE BEAUTIFUL

ANNIE LAURIE

Words by William Douglas
(To a Scottish melody)

SWEET MOLLY MALONE

Irish Folk Song

SHE'LL BE COMIN' 'ROUND THE MOUNTAIN

American
Folk Song

PASTIME

From a collection of
17th Century court music.

GAVOTTE AMARILLIS

Traditional British melody
(17th Century)

PRINCE RUPERT'S MARCH

From Ballet "THE DANCE MASTER"
(17th century)

WHEN I DREAM OF LOVE

TRADITIONAL BRITISH SONG
(circa 1650)

DULCINA

TRADITIONAL BRITISH
(circa 1720)

Alto

Tenor

A HEART AT EASE

From Ballet "THE DANCE MASTER"
(17th century)

Alto

Tenor

A LOVER AND HIS LASS

THOMAS MORLEY
(1557-1603)

TRIOS FOR SOPRANO, ALTO and TENOR

DRINK TO ME ONLY WITH THINE EYES

ENGLISH TRADITIONAL
(circa 1770)

O DEAR, WHAT CAN THE MATTER BE?

ENGLISH FOLK SONG
(18th century)

OIL OF BARLEY

From ballet "THE DANCE MASTER"
(1650)

OLD KING COLE

ENGLISH TRADITIONAL

LADY FAIR

ENGLISH TRADITIONAL
(circa 1730)

MELODY OF MAY

From "THE BEGGAR'S OPERA"
(circa 1728)

TOBACCO'S BUT AN INDIAN WEED

ENGLISH TRADITIONAL

THREE RAVENS

ENGLISH TRADITIONAL

74

SLEEP, SWEET MUSE

ROBERT JONES
(16th century)

THE WILLOW

ENGLISH TRADITIONAL

COME AND KISS ME NOW

ENGLISH TRADITIONAL

SORRY AM I TO HAVE LOVED

ENGLISH TRADITIONAL

IRISH COUNTRY DANCE

From "THE DANCE MASTER"
(British ballet, circa 1650)

PACKINGTON'S PARTY

TRADITIONAL IRISH TUNE

REVIVE THY WEARY SPIRIT

ELIZABETH ROGERS
(circa 1666)

A FRIEND A FOE MAY BE

From "THE DANCE MASTER"
(British ballet, circa 1650)

MAD ROBIN

From "THE DANCE MASTER"
(British ballet, circa 1650)

TERZETTO

FRANZ WASNER
(18th century)

ENSEMBLE SELECTIONS

(For Soprano, Alto, Tenor and Bass)

SPRING REVERIE

THOMAS CAMPION
(1567-1620)

O MISTRESS MINE

WILLIAM BYRD
(17th century)

SO, MY LOVE, GOOD-NIGHT

ELIZABETH ROGERS
(17th century)

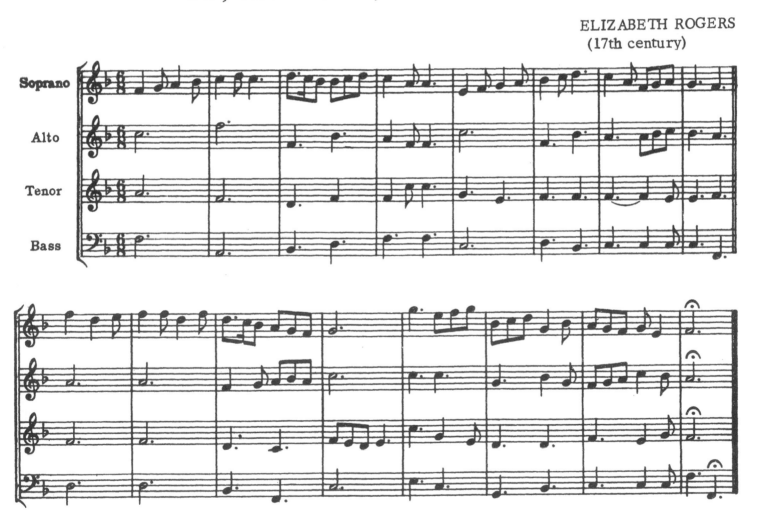

GOD REST YE MERRY, GENTLEMEN

TRADITIONAL CHRISTMAS CAROL
(Probably 17th century)

EARLY IN THE MORNING

TRADITIONAL ENGLISH
(Probably 18th century)

MYSTERIOSO

From "THE BEGGAR'S OPERA" (British)
(circa 1728)

Soprano
Alto
Tenor
Bass

KNIGHT OF THE GARTER

From British ballet "THE DANCE MASTER"

Soprano
Alto
Tenor
Bass

SINCE FIRST I SAW THY FACE

THOMAS FORD
(1580-1648)

HAPPILY FLOWS THE ALE

WILLIAM BYRD
(17th century)

THE BRITISH GRENADIERS

ENGLISH TRADITIONAL

FORTUNE IS MY FOE

WILLIAM BYRD
(17th century)

ONCE AGAIN, MY DEAREST

JOHN DOWLAND
(1563-1626)

LOVE ME FOR MYSELF ALONE

PHILIP ROSSETER
(1575-1623)

WHEN THE STARS ARE SHINING

16th Century German tune

LORD WILLOUGHBY

WILLIAM BYRD
(17th century)

BLESSED ARE THE SHEPHERDS

HENRY PURCELL
(1658-1695)

Embellishments

Advanced players will frequently embellish their performances with special effects or "embellishments" whether or not they are indicated in the music notation.

The most popular of these is the TRILL formed by rapid repeat pressing of the "trill finger" designated in the samples below by the sign *tr* , while holding the other fingers in place.

The fingering may vary on different recorders, and it may require some experimenting to get a trill effect.   Trills usually start on the tone above the one notated.   The following are a number of sample trills for Soprano C Recorder and for Alto F Recorder:

All fingering is Baroque unless noted with "G" for German fingering.

SOPRANO RECORDERS:

ALTO RECORDERS:

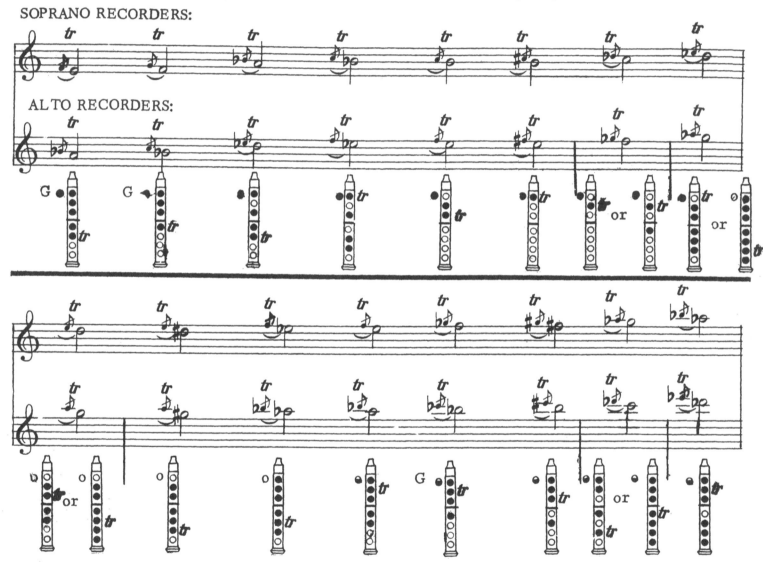

SAMPLES OF VARIOUS ORNAMENTS OR EMBELLISHMENTS

Appoggiatura	Inverted Mordent	Trill (sample)		Mordent	Turn
As written	As written	As written		As written	As written
As played	As played	As played		As played	As played